KIDS LEARNING SPANISH OUT LOUD

Children's Learn Spanish Books

Speedy Publishing LLC
40 E. Main St. #1156
Newark, DE 19711
www.speedypublishing.com

LEARN
SPANISH
SANGRIA

AGUJA
A
BÚHO
B
CHOCOLATE
Ch
CONEJO
C

ALFABETOS ESPAÑOLAS

Spanish Alphabet

SPANISH	ENGLISH
Aguja	Needle
Búho	Owl
Conejo	Rabbit
Chocolate	Chocolate

D
DINOSAURIO
ERIZO
E
FLOR
F
GANSO
G

ALFABETOS ESPAÑOLAS

Spanish Alphabet

SPANISH	ENGLISH
Dinosauro	Dinosaur
Erizo	Hedgehog
Flor	Flower
Ganso	Goose

HORMIGA
H
I
INTERROGACIÓN
J
JIRAFA
KIWI
K

ALFABETOS ESPAÑOLAS

Spanish Alphabet

SPANISH	ENGLISH
Hormiga	Ant
Interogacion	Question
Jirafa	Giraffe
Kiwi	Kiwi

LIMON
L
LA LLAVE
Ll
MONO
M
N
NARANJA

ALFABETOS ESPAÑOLAS

Spanish Alphabet

SPANISH	ENGLISH
Limon	Lemon
La Llave	The Key
Mono	Monkey
Naranja	Orange

ÑU
Ñ
OVEJA
O
P
PIÑA
QUESO
Q

ALFABETOS ESPAÑOLAS

Spanish Alphabet

SPANISH	ENGLISH
Ñu	Wildebeest
Oveja	Sheep
Piña	Pineapple
Queso	Cheese

SETA
S
RANA
R
TAZA
T

ALFABETOS ESPAÑOLAS

Spanish Alphabet

SPANISH	ENGLISH
Rana	Frog
Seta	Mushroom
Taza	Cup

UVAS
U
VERDURAS
V
WAFLES
W

ALFABETOS ESPAÑOLAS

Spanish Alphabet

SPANISH	ENGLISH
Uwas	Uwa
Verduras	Vegetables
Wafles	Waffles

X
XYLÓPHONE
Z
ZANAHORIA
YOGUR
Y

ALFABETOS ESPAÑOLAS

Spanish Alphabet

SPANISH	ENGLISH
Xylophone	Xylophone
Yogurt	Yoghurt
Zanahoria	Carrot

NUMÉROS DE COMPTAGE 1-20

Counting numbers 1-10

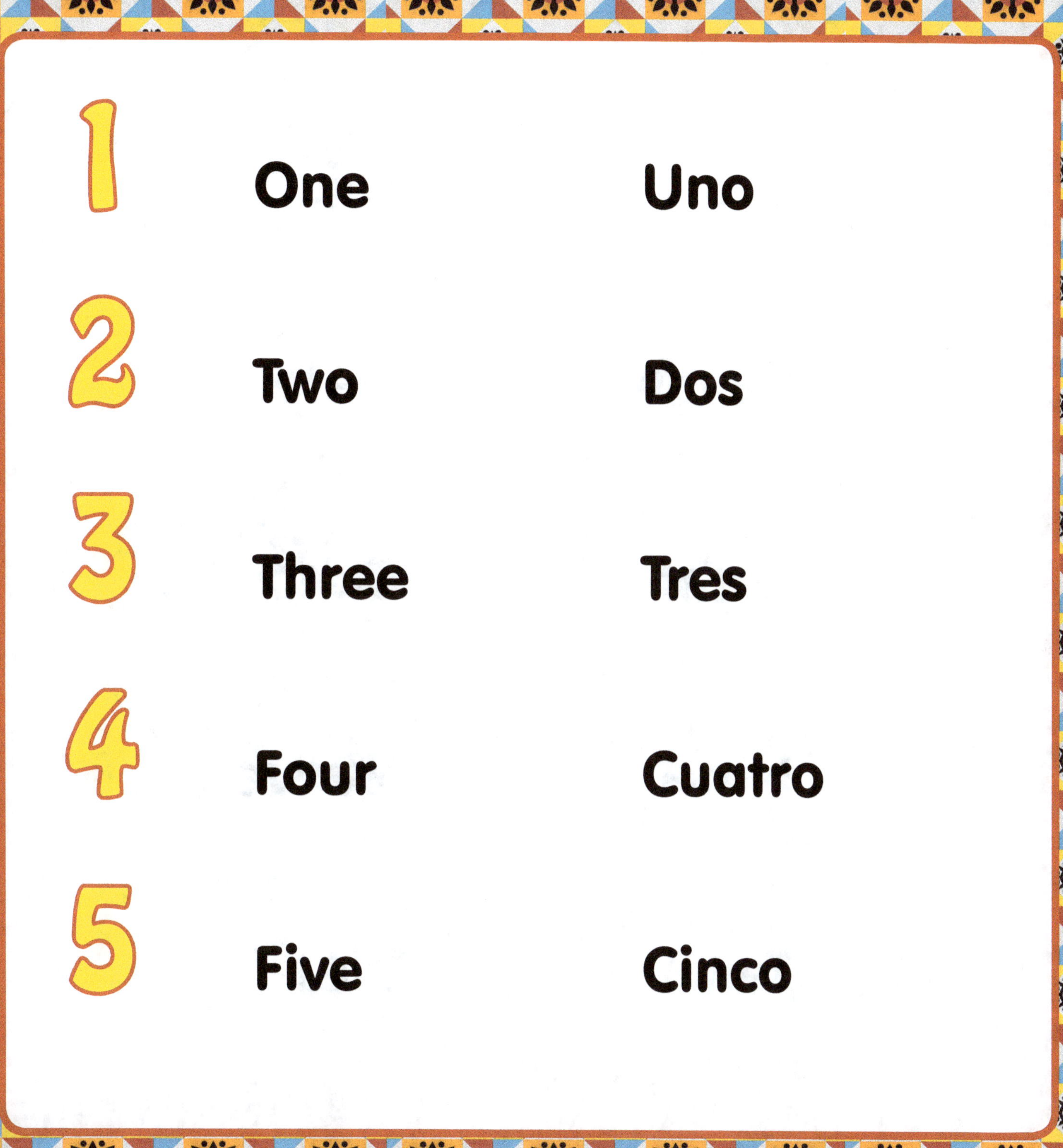

1	One	Uno
2	Two	Dos
3	Three	Tres
4	Four	Cuatro
5	Five	Cinco

6	Six	Seis
7	Seven	Siete
8	Eight	Ocho
9	Nine	Nueve
10	Ten	Diez

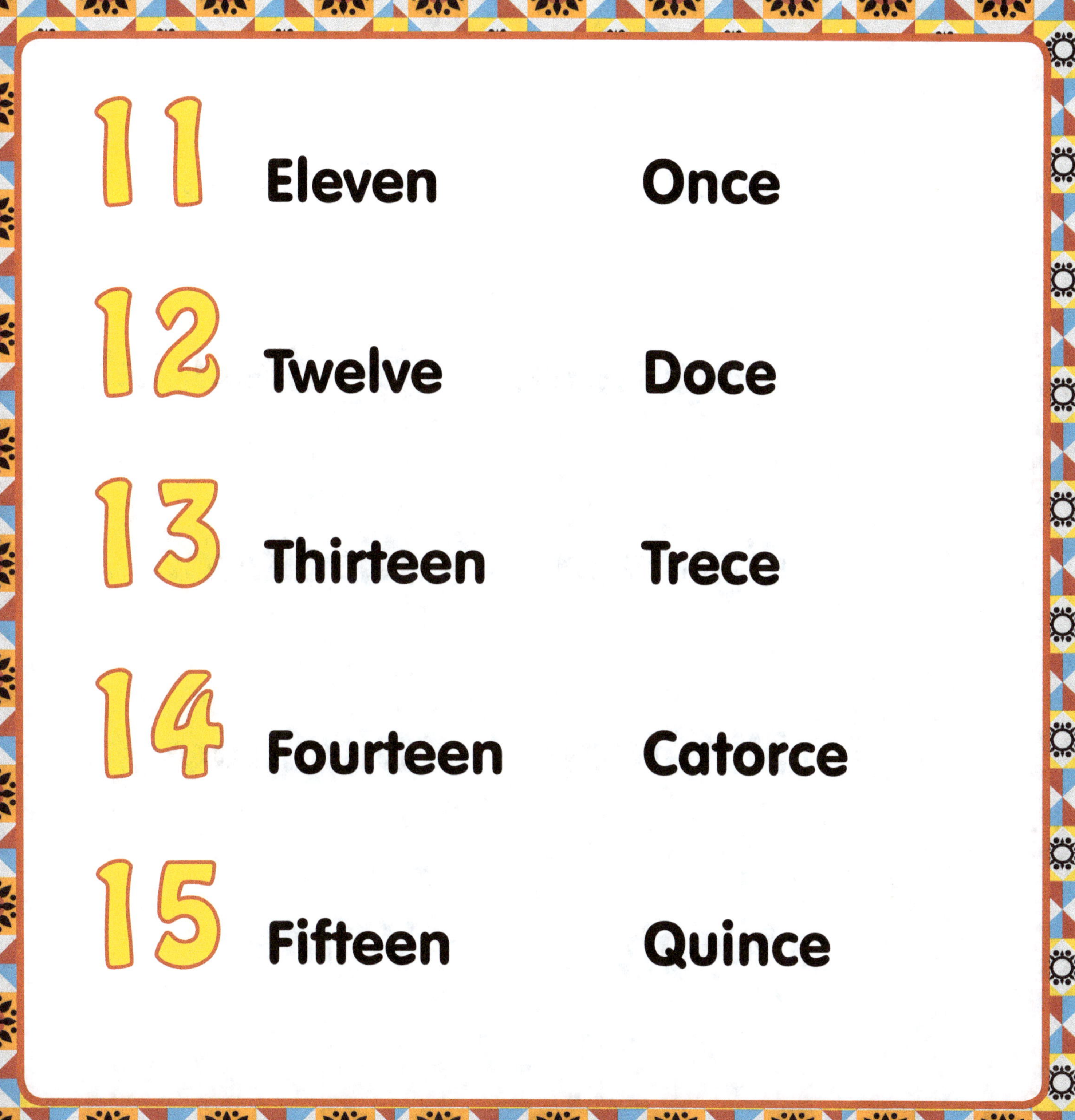

11	Eleven	Once
12	Twelve	Doce
13	Thirteen	Trece
14	Fourteen	Catorce
15	Fifteen	Quince

16	Sixteen	Dieciséis
17	Seventeen	De diecisiete
18	Eighteen	Dieciocho
19	Nineteen	Diecinueve
20	Twenty	Veinte

CUT AND PASTE!

Cut the Spanish term and paste it beside the English term.

	English	Spanish
6	Six	
2	Two	
8	Eight	
20	Twenty	

Ocho

Veinte

Seis

Doz

For Cutting purposes only

CUT AND PASTE!

Cut the Spanish term and paste it beside the English term.

	English	Spanish
	Fifteen	
	Nine	
	Eleven	
	Three	

Nueve

Once

Tres

Quince

CUT AND PASTE!

Cut the Spanish term and paste it beside the English term.

	English	Spanish
	One	
	Ten	
	Seven	
	Eight	

Un

Dix

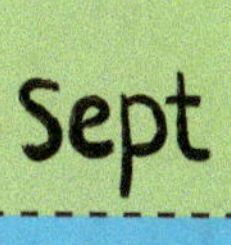

Douze

For Cutting purposes only

CUT AND PASTE!

Cut the Spanish term and paste it beside the English term.

	English	Spanish
	Seventeen	
14	Fourteen	
5	Five	
	Sixteen	

Catorce

Dieciséis

Cinco

De diecisiete

CUT AND PASTE!

Cut the Spanish term and paste it beside the English term.

English	Spanish
 Thirteen	
 Eighteen	
 Nineteen	
 Four	

Dieciocho

Trece

cuatro

Diecinueve

LOS COLORES EN ESPAÑOL

Colors in Spanish

YELLOW
jaune
BLUE
bleu
RED
rouge
FRENCH
ENGLISH
yellow
amarillo
blue
azul
red
rojo

GREEN
vert
VIOLET
violet
ORANGE
orange
FRENCH
ENGLISH
green
verde
Violet
Violeta
orange
anaranjado

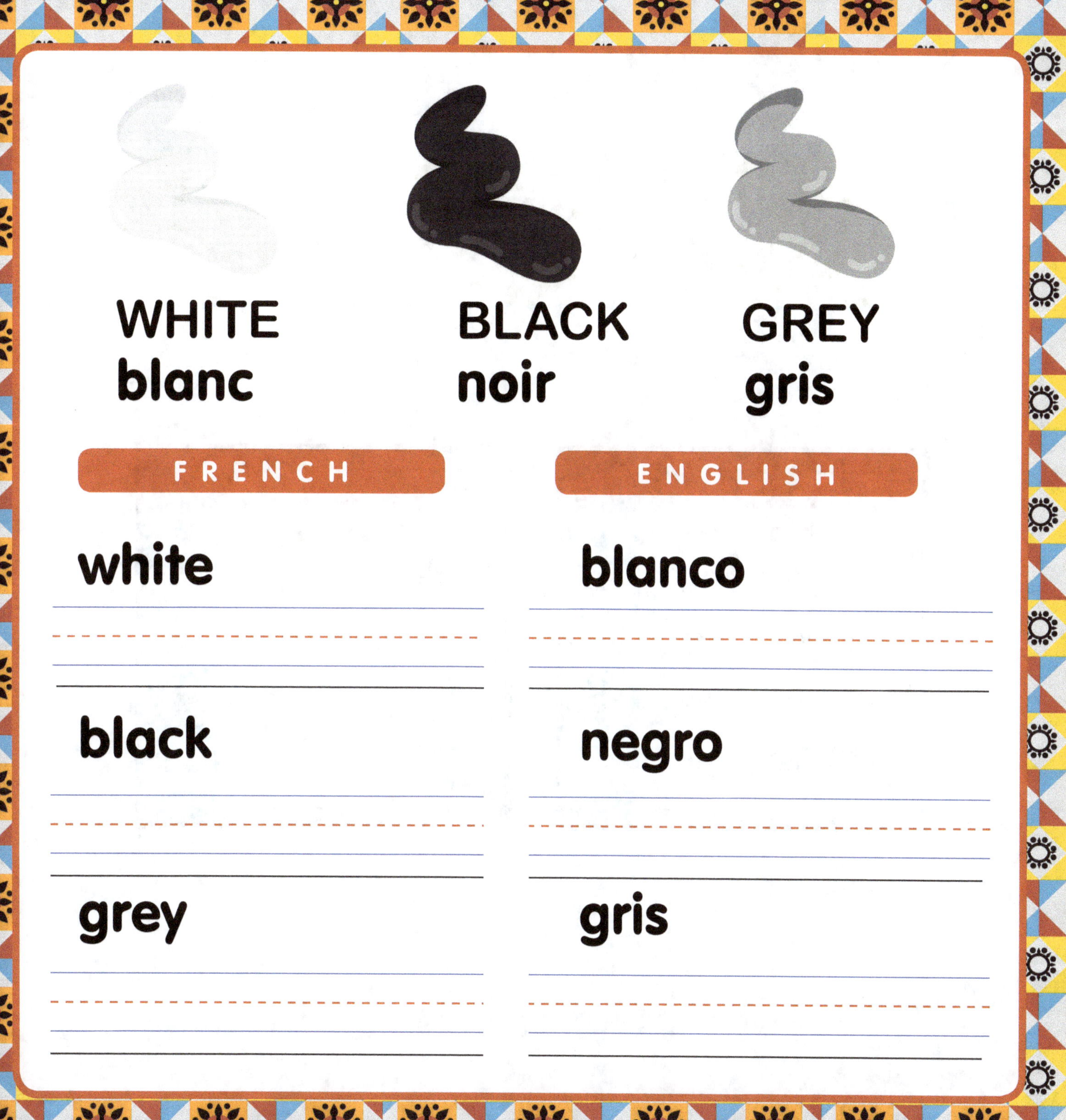

WHITE
blanc

BLACK
noir

GREY
gris

FRENCH	ENGLISH
white	**blanco**
black	**negro**
grey	**gris**

ANSWER KEY

CUT AND PASTE!
Cut the Spanish term and paste it beside the English term.
English
Spanish
Six
Seis
Two
Doz
Eight
Ocho
Twenty
Veinte
Ocho
Veinte
Seis
Doz

CUT AND PASTE!
Cut the Spanish term and paste it beside the English term.
English
Spanish
Fifteen
Quince
Nine
Nueve
Eleven
Once
Three
Tres
Nueve
Once
Tres
Quince

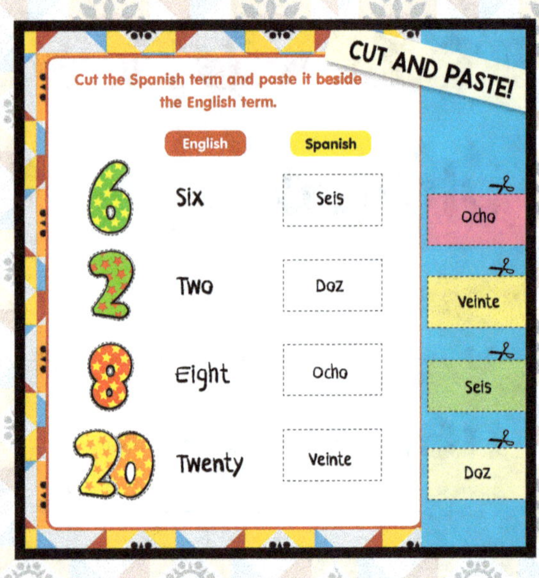

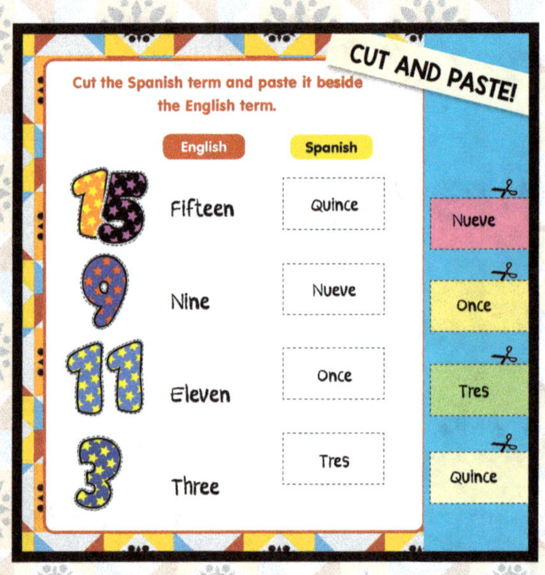

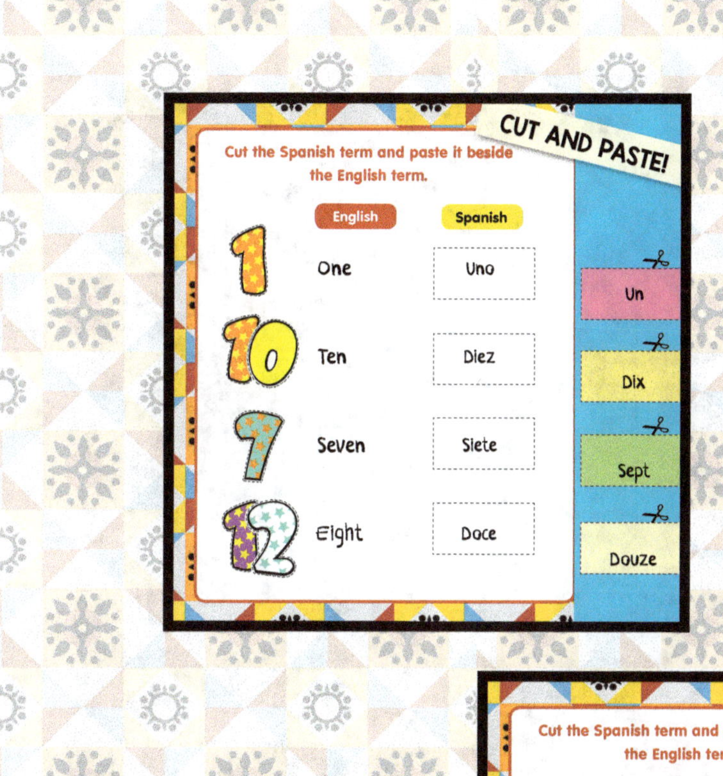
CUT AND PASTE!
Cut the Spanish term and paste it beside the English term.
English
Spanish
1
One
Uno
10
Ten
Diez
7
Seven
Siete
12
Eight
Doce
Un
Dix
Sept
Douze

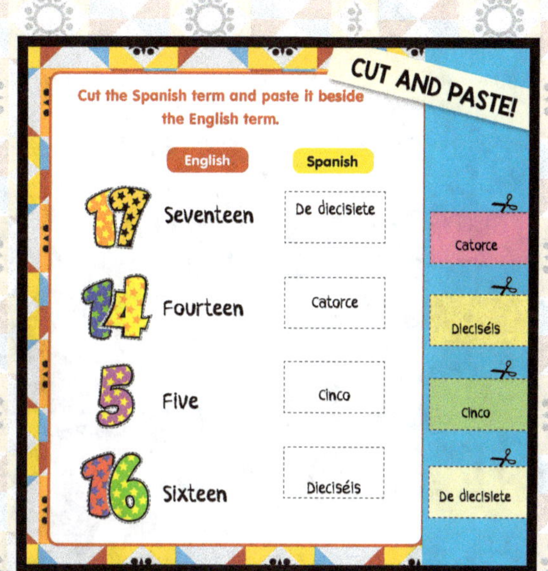
CUT AND PASTE!
Cut the Spanish term and paste it beside the English term.
English
Spanish
17
Seventeen
De diecisiete
14
Fourteen
Catorce
5
Five
Cinco
16
Sixteen
Dieciséis
Catorce
Dieciséis
Cinco
De diecisiete

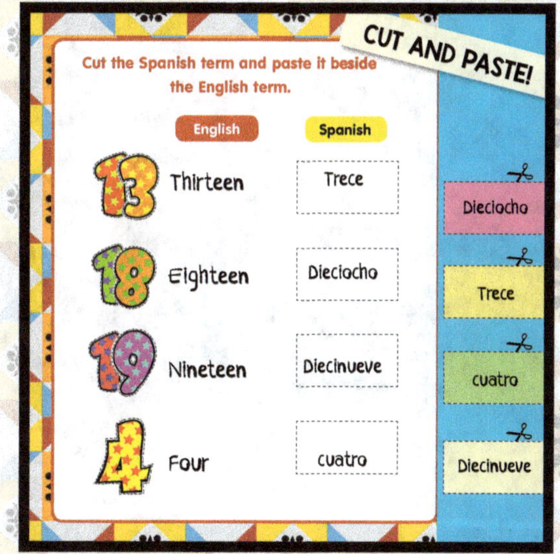
CUT AND PASTE!
Cut the Spanish term and paste it beside the English term.
English
Spanish
13
Thirteen
Trece
18
Eighteen
Dieciocho
19
Nineteen
Diecinueve
4
Four
cuatro
Dieciocho
Trece
cuatro
Diecinueve

Visit
BABY PROFESSOR
EDUCATION KIDS
www.BabyProfessorBooks.com
to download Free Baby Professor eBooks
and view our catalog of new and exciting
Children's Books

www.ingramcontent.com/pod-product-compliance
Lightning Source LLC
LaVergne TN
LVHW060512170826
845677LV00026B/1720

* 9 7 9 8 8 6 9 4 4 5 0 4 9 *